USING THIS BOOK

One of the best ways of helping children read is to read stories to them and with them.

If you have been reading earlier books in this series, you will be used to reading the story from the left-hand pages only, with words and sentences under the illustrations for the children to read.

In this book, **the story is printed on both the left- and right-hand pages.**

The first time you read the book, read the **whole** story, **both** left- and right-hand pages, aloud to the child and look at the illustrations together.

The next time the book is read, you read the text on the left-hand page and the child, in turn, reads the text on the right-hand page, and so on through the book.

LADYBIRD BOOKS, INC.
Lewiston, Maine 04240 U.S.A.
© Text and layout SHEILA McCULLAGH MCMLXXXV
© In publication LADYBIRD BOOKS LTD MCMLXXXV
Loughborough, Leicestershire, England

Printed in England

The Sandalwood Girl

written by SHEILA McCULLAGH
illustrated by JON DAVIS

This book belongs to:

Ladybird Books

There was once a very old house.
It stood in a big, wild garden,
at the end of Puddle Lane.
A magician lived in an attic room
under the roof, but the rest
of the house was empty.
That is, it was empty
except for some old toys.

The toys had been left behind
in an empty attic room.

When the people moved out
of the house, they had forgotten
all about the toys.
There was a clown, and a monkey,
and three or four puppets from
an old toy theater.
There was a rocking horse and
a young lion cub.
They all lay there in the dust.

A wooden girl sat on
a dusty shelf by the window.
She was made of sandalwood.

Children had once loved to play
with her, but no one ever came
to play with her now.
The sandalwood girl was very lonely.
She stared out of the dusty window
at the tree that grew outside.
Sometimes, birds flew into the tree.
Sometimes, she saw cats climbing up it.
But they never came into the attic,
and the sandalwood girl grew very sad.
One night, when the moon
was shining down,
and the wind was blowing hard,
the window fell open.

A big barn owl flew in
through the window.
The owl had been out
all night in the wind.
He flew down onto a shelf
near the sandalwood girl, and
he went to sleep.

The owl slept on the shelf all day.
When night came, he flew out
of the attic again.
After that, he came back often
to sleep on the shelf.
The sandalwood girl couldn't talk,
but she was very glad to see him.
The days didn't seem quite so long,
with the barn owl sleeping there.

There was a clock on the roof
of the old house.
An iron boy stood by the clock.

The iron boy rang the hours.
He struck the bell with a silver hammer,
so that everyone knew what time it was.

One night, the moon
was shining down.
The sandalwood girl
was sitting on the shelf.

The sandalwood girl was feeling
very lonely.
The owl was away, hunting.
She heard the iron boy strike the hours:
six, seven, eight, nine, ten, eleven.
At twelve o'clock, she was still
listening. She was waiting for
the iron boy to strike midnight.
She heard the iron boy begin
to strike the bell.

One, two, three, four, five, six,
seven, eight, nine, ten, eleven,
twelve — thirteen!
The iron boy had struck the bell
thirteen times!

The sandalwood girl was so surprised,
that she sat up.
And then she was even more surprised,
to find that she **could** sit up!

She tried to move her arms—
and she **could** move her arms!
She tried to move her legs—
and she **could** move her legs!
She tried to stand up—
and she **could** stand up!

The sandalwood girl stepped
to the edge of the shelf.
She leaned out, to look over
the edge —
and she fell off the shelf.

She fell onto the dusty floor.
She lay there for a moment,
looking up at the window.

The sandalwood girl hadn't hurt herself,
and she hadn't broken anything.
After a moment, she got up,
and looked all around.
The door of the room was open.

"Come in," said the old man.
"Come in. You've just missed
meeting the iron boy.
The iron boy has just gone."

The sandalwood girl walked across
to the open door.
(Her legs were very stiff,
but she found that she **could** walk.)
She looked around the door.

The sandalwood girl saw
an empty hall.
At the end of the hall,
there was another door.
A light was shining under it, and
the door was open a little way.
The sandalwood girl walked slowly
down the hall.
(She wasn't used to walking, and
she still walked very stiffly.)

She came to the do
of the other room.
She opened the doc
An old man was sit
in a chair by the fir
He looked up, and s
the sandalwood gir

The sandalwood girl went
into the room.
"Are you the Magician?"
she asked.
"Yes, I'm the Magician,"
said the old man.
"What can I do for you?"

The sandalwood girl looked
at the Magician.
He sounded very gruff,
but he looked very kind.
"Please help me," she whispered.
"Please help me.
I've been sitting on a shelf
for years and years.
When the clock struck thirteen,
I found that I could move.
I can talk to you, too.
But I want to be really alive!
I want to be free."

The Magician looked
at the sandalwood girl.
"You want to be free?" he asked.
"Yes," said the sandalwood girl.
"I want to be free,
and I want to be really alive."

"Are you sure?" asked the Magician.
"The world is a dangerous place.
You're safe, here in this house.
You can walk around, and talk to me.
You won't be lonely any more.
Do you really want to be free?"

"I want to be free,"
said the sandalwood girl.
"I want to be free."

The Magician sighed.

"I want to grow up,"
said the sandalwood girl.
"I want to be really alive."

The Magician shook his head.
"It will be very difficult,"
he said.
"I don't care," said the sandalwood girl.
"I don't care how difficult it is."

"All right," said the Magician.
"I can't make you really alive myself—
not more alive than you are now.
But I can tell you what you must do."

"Please tell me,"
said the sandalwood girl.

"You will have to go away,"
said the Magician.
"You will have to go
a long way away."

31

"I will go anywhere,"
said the sandalwood girl.
"Then you must take a long journey,"
said the Magician.
"A long way away from here,
there is a country called Zorn.
It is a magical country.
You must go to the Country of Zorn,
and find your way to the Blue Mountains.
High up in the Blue Mountains,
you will find the Silver River.
If you bathe in the Silver River,
you will become really alive."

"How can I get there?"
asked the sandalwood girl.
"How can I find the way?"

"I know a big barn owl,"
said the Magician.
"He's a friend of mine. He knows
the way to the Country of Zorn.
He'll take you."
"A big barn owl sometimes sleeps
on a shelf in the attic,"
said the sandalwood girl.
"That's the one," said the Magician.
"He told me he was sleeping there.
I'll call him, if you like.
But are you **sure** you want to go?
It will be a dangerous journey.
You would be much safer,
if you stayed here with me."

"You are very kind,
but I must go,"
said the sandalwood girl.
"Can I go now?"

The Magician sighed.
"That's what the iron boy said—
the iron boy, who struck the bell.
He's gone to the Country of Zorn.
You may meet him there.
Well, if you really want to go,
I will call the barn owl."

"I'm ready,"
said the sandalwood girl.
"But before I go,
please tell me my name."

"You don't have a name,"
said the Magician.
"If you ever had one,
I've forgotten it.
But it doesn't matter.
You'll find a name
in the Country of Zorn."

The Magician got up.
He went to the window,
and opened it.
He gave a long, low call.

The big owl came flying
in through the window. He landed
on the back of the Magician's chair.
The Magician stood up.
"Welcome, barn owl," he said.
"I have something for you to do.
You must take this sandalwood girl
to the Country of Zorn.
She wants to be really alive.
She wants to grow up.
Set her down safely,
at the edge of the Country of Zorn,
and come back to me."
The Magician picked up
the sandalwood girl, and put her
carefully on the owl's back.
"Hold on tight, sandalwood girl!"
he said. "Goodbye, and may good luck
go with you."
The barn owl spread his wings.

He flew out the open window,
with the sandalwood girl
on his back.

They flew over the houses,
and over the trees,
over the hills,
and under the stars,
until at last they came
to the Country of Zorn.

Then the owl flew
down to the ground,
and the sandalwood girl
got off his back.

"You must find your own way now,"
said the owl. "You must find
your own way to the Blue Mountains.
I must fly back to the Magician."

"I will," said the sandalwood girl.
"Thank you, barn owl.
I will never forget you."

"And I will never forget you,"
said the owl.

The owl lifted his wings,
and flew away, under the stars.
The sandalwood girl looked
at the trees and the hills.
''I am in the Country of Zorn,''
she said.
''I am in the Country of Zorn.
I will find my way
to the Blue Mountains.
And then I will be really alive.''